Tyrtaeus Bailey, William James

Martial Fragments of Tyrtaeus

Tyrtaeus Bailey, William James

Martial Fragments of Tyrtaeus

ISBN/EAN: 9783743350007

Manufactured in Europe, USA, Canada, Australia, Japa

Cover: Foto ©ninafisch / pixelio.de

Manufactured and distributed by brebook publishing software
(www.brebook.com)

Tyrtaeus Bailey, William James

Martial Fragments of Tyrtaeus

MARTIAL FRAGMENTS,

ETC.

MARTIAL FRAGMENTS

OF

TYRTÆUS,

TRANSLATED INTO ENGLISH VERSE.

WITH

A Martial Elegy

ON

THE DEMISE OF H.R.H. PRINCE ALBERT;

ETC.

BY

JAMES W. BAILEY.

London:

HARRISON, 59, PALL MALL.

Bookseller to the Queen.

MDCCCLXII.

[PRICE 2s. 6D.]

TO

THE RIGHT HONOURABLE

LORD VISCOUNT PALMERSTON, K.G.,

ETC., ETC.,

AND

THE BRITISH VOLUNTEERS,

This little Volume

IS

DEDICATED,

AS

A SLIGHT TOKEN OF ADMIRATION AND RESPECT,

BY

THE TRANSLATOR.

LONDON, MDCCCLXI.

ADVERTISEMENT.

THE British public, ever disposed to patronize the endeavours of the humble aspirant to its favour, will not, it is trusted, regard with asperity or surprise the following attempt at a new translation of four of the noblest fragments which have been left to us by a remote antiquity. And if only a small portion of the spirit and fire of the fine originals shall have been conveyed to and infused in the present version of Martial Fragments of Tyrtæus, the translator will venture to hope, after having offered the apology due on account of his boldness or temerity, that he will be permitted to escape with but slight reprehension.

INTRODUCTORY REMARKS.

THE general reader or tyro may be pleased to be reminded, from the pages of Grecian history, that Tyrtæus* was an Athenian poet, who flourished about the year B.C. 682, Olymp. XXIV. At this period the Spartans, in the second war with their rivals the Messenians, experienced defeats and disasters, and having known what it is to have an invader in the land, applied, in consequence of an oracular injunction, to the Athenian state *for a general*. That state, it has been said, deeming the affairs of the Spartans hopeless, sent them in derision a poet, a schoolmaster, one that halted—in short—Tyrtæus !

Now the poetical genius has often shone forth in the warrior ; the " son of song" too has seldom been slow to take his stand in the foremost ranks of those who defend liberty or their country's weal ; a natural defect, similar to that alluded to, in no wise impaired the lustre of the name of that poet, whom a most high authority has pronounced " the most eminent in the present century." To which opinion we unhesita-

* See Smith's Biographical Dictionary, *article* ' Tyrtæus.'

tingly bend; whilst an affectionate regard for passages unmatched, save in Homer and in Tyrtæus, permits us not to forget who followed close behind, viz. the author of Marmion.

In favour of the schoolmaster's profession, at least as regards the respect paid to it in the present age, the same authority is quoted :—" It is admitted by all that the career of those who instruct and form the youth of this country is one eminently deserving the respect and esteem of their fellow-countrymen ; for the strength of a nation consists not so much in the numbers of the people as in the character of the men."* Again, elsewhere :—" instructors of youth—a most valuable class of society, men upon whose exertions depends the whole success of a nation, because, unless the people have their minds cultivated and stored with knowledge, it is plain that for all great purposes they are almost as if they were not."†

In the semi-mythical account of Tyrtæus, however, a reasonable surmise would merely point to the probability of his having imparted casual instruction in the art he practised, a habit by no means foreign to the simple manners of the ancients. But we are aware that respect for a superior and deferential awe to age were ever most highly characteristic of Spartan virtue. We are also well aware that the most prominent man of this age was formerly not considered to be gifted with any very extraordinary military qualifi-

---

*v. Lord Palmerston's Speech at Harrow on the occasion of laying the foundation-stone of the Vaughan Library.

†v. Lord Palmerston's Speech at Southampton on *Competitive Examinations.*

cations. Might not, then, Tyrtæus, without incurring ridicule, even though actually a schoolmaster, a poet, lame, and what not besides ; having, according to the institutions of his country, been trained in the gymnastic schools, where manly exercises were appointed by public masters, and subject to a discipline no less severe than that of Sparta ; and having served the usual apprenticeship in arms, which consisted in being " sent into the country, to keep watch and ward in the towns and fortresses on the coast and frontier, and to perform any other tasks which might be imposed upon him for the protection of Attica ;"* have failed to display at the onset those qualities which sometimes prognosticate the future brilliant soldier ? At any rate he challenged from the Spartan phalanxes singular respect, if not veneration, on account of high talents, which, if not immediately manifested in the service of Athens, soon wrought a favourable change for the Spartans, when brought into play, both in the council and on the field.

The Spartans ultimately becoming victorious over their enemies by means of the military instructions of the Athenian, and stirred up (as was our own Sir Philip Sidney on hearing the old ballad on Chevy Chase sung) by his elegies or panegyrics on martial spirit and personal valour, the mission of Tyrtæus resulted to him in the acquisition of the rights and privileges of Spartan citizenship, and in the enjoyment of a celebrated reputation. In coupling his name with that of the " father of Poetry" Horace has conferred the highest commendation :—

*v. Thirlwall's History of Greece, vol. ii. p. 57.

" Post hos insignis Homerus,
Tyrtæusque mares animos in Martia bella
Versibus exacuit."

Quintilian also :—" Quid? Horatius frustra Tyrtæum Homero subjunxit ?"

The war-elegies of Tyrtæus, which anciently comprised five books, were prescribed as permanent recitations by the republic of Lacedæmon. Judging from the few remains, they must have been admirably suited to the Spartan tyro. Free from the stain which the vehicle of instruction so often leaves upon the unsuspecting and less robust mind of unguarded youth, the fragments of Tyrtæus, which scarcely number one hundred and fifty lines, abound with the loftiest sentiments. In them the love of country—of freedom—of valour — of magnanimity — the sanctity of helpless innocence—the glory of nobly dying in its defence, are inculcated with " thoughts that breathe and words that burn." In them no act of aggression, of savagely making an inroad into another's country, nor a prodigious slaughter, nor revengeful feeling, find any praise.

Several excellent poetical versions of fragments of Tyrtæus have, from time to time, under various aspects, been presented to the English reader. One printed in London for Tho. Payne, 1761 ; another by Pye in 1795 ; and Polwhele's well-known translation, need particular enumeration. Also a spirited but not strict version, dated London, 1804, and University Press, Edinburgh, 1807, with the following appropriate dedication :—

" To the Martial Bands of the Britons, armed, and arming, to defend, on British Ground, the Honour, the

Liberty, the Laws, the Hearths, and the Altars, of the British Empire ; these MARTIAL EFFUSIONS are inscribed, with ardent wishes for Safety, Success, and Glory, by the Translator."

In this warlike age, when the world abroad seems "bristling" (as the phrase is) with new - fashioned bayonets ; and man's highest talents are strained to improve and invent the swiftest, surest, and most powerful means for his own destruction ; whilst England, "calm as the glassy ocean" where she rides, eyes with confidence her great premier ; it was thought with much deference that a more literal metrical version than has hitherto appeared (and one adapted for the use of the elocutionist) might not prove unacceptable to " the youth of England." For " a manly determination to protect and maintain what we have "* has entered the breasts of all, and not one is ambitious to exceed his simple duty.

In this country where men " try to raise the level on which they stand, not by pulling others down, but by elevating themselves,"† it were needless to admonish or caution our youth against too much imbibing " that military ardour and that high estimate of the dispositions and talents necessary to success in war, which, although they may never carry him into the field, will nevertheless engage his feelings, and even his opinions, in the support of a system of bloodshed."‡ The expedition of the deputation from the Society of Friends to

* Lord Palmerston. v. Times (Friday), Sept. 6, 1861.
† v. Lord Palmerston's Speech at Southampton.
‡ v. Preface to Peace-Reading Book ; edited by H. G. Adams, 1844.

the throne of All the Russias presented au act more
worthy of imitation than aught else which happened
during the warfare which ensued. And the letter
addressed more recently by the Emperor of Russia
himself to the American hosts was surely dictated by a
most happy tone of mind. Even the act of the Five
Liverpool Merchants, rife as it was with the highest
impropriety in respect of *etiquette*, though laughed
down, will yet be designated by the reflecting and
right-minded man, as infinitely to be preferred to the
doubtful glory of many a well-fought field.

Whilst obedient to the divine behest to " agree with
thine adversary quickly," which is by no means in-
compatible with steps of precaution, and active and
prudent measures for prevention of mischief, it may be
well that the rising generation, and even a distant
posterity likewise, remember with mingled feelings of
Christian humility and national pride "that the principle of arbitration which the British Government, to
its great honour, was the first to commend to the
attention of the Paris Conference in 1854, through the
mouth of Lord Clarendon, was recognized and ratified
by the unanimous consent of that august body, and
embodied in a resolution expressed in the following
terms :—

" The Plenipotentiaries do not hesitate to express,
in the name of their Governments, the wish that
States between which any serious misunderstanding
may arise, should, before appealing to arms, have
recourse, as far as circumstances might allow, to the
good offices of a friendly Power."*

The principle, thus formally consecrated by the sanction of all the great Governments of Europe, having since received the spontaneous and cordial homage of eminent statesmen of this country of various political parties, has been rightly designated as a "great triumph, a powerful engine on behalf of civilization and humanity." "It recognises and establishes," to use the words of the Earl of Malmesbury, "the truth, that time, by giving place for reason to operate, is as much a preventive as a healer of hostilities."

Much as the principle of war is to be decried; and our greatest generals have abominated it most; the feeling of patriotism, which has in all ages commanded the highest admiration of mankind, and been extolled, cannot be too warmly cherished. For a definition of this word 'patriotism' no British heart is ever at a loss when appealed to. And it is not in the writings of the ancients only that this glorious spirit shines. The accomplished reader will experience no difficulty in discovering in the literary or oratorical* productions of his own country all that is calculated to awaken "martial" or patriotic feelings: where the latter fail to predominate, the battle degenerates into a mere combat of tigers.

Illustrative of martial minstrelsy, we shall only cite the famous "Scots wha hae wi' Wallace bled," &c.; Byron's "Sons of the Greeks, arise," and the "Rhyfelgyrch Gwyr Harlech" (March of the Men of Harlech),

---

* Read that immortal speech delivered by Lord Lyndhurst, which concludes with the words "Væ Victis!"

with its fine Welsh air, as sung at the present time to listening thousands, with marked enthusiasm. We will introduce, however, for the perusal of our more youthful readers, a slight production by W. W., 1832 (then in the thirteenth year of his age), as afterwards put by him into an antiquated form. It is fair to say he had not then read Tyrtæus.

WAR SONG.

MENNE at armes, be not afraid,
Fear vaileth nouzt, and ye han plaid
An ydle time, God wot, so long,
Nowth hear your mynstreles battaile song.

5 The foemen comen, we must go
Against them miztily, I tro ;
They would our Ynglond fromm us take,
And us whan conquerde would slaves make.

But wol we bide them ? No ! then fizt
10 Wyd al our strength, wyd al our mizt.
God sped us al ! we stynt ne blame,
Till eche blood drop be fro us gane.

O whare the vse to lead our lyf
Sister to sloth, straunger to stryf?
15 'Bet is to lede our lyf iu fame,
And, dying, leave behind grete name.

Know, warriors, ye most die som day,
Know, next minute, som happen may ;
Lyf is incertain to every beast and man,
20 Therefor let die as bravelich as we can.

Die not like peple in soft bed,
Who on smal pain grete teres shed,
Rizt thus they don, and coward grane,
Ne die lich us on the grene plain.

25 Fizt wel, and peraunter som may
Rise hie for feat of armes to-day :
Bear in your mind, and stronglich think,
'If ye do spyl, Ynglond wol sink.'

Lo ! yon the fomen come in syzt ;
30 We wol ere long put them to flyzt.
God save our king ! nowth fast lay on ;
Ring, trompes, on high, sound, claryon !

In fine, be we or be we not "on the eve of great
events," as it is worded, the world will still perceive
that, arisen as this Christian country has by arduous
paths to its present unexampled magnificence and in-
creasing power, pace has been kept with the require-
ments of the age, the powerful arm hath been meted,
our own shortcomings weighed. And a memorable
opportunity has presented itself for making a brilliant
display of love for 'fatherland.' Happy is that volun-
teer, who from purely unselfish patriotic motives
"girded himself in his strength," and so enshrined
himself in the hearts of the aged and of the beautiful
of these isles ! Even happier is the sire, who, having
served his sovereign upwards of fifty years since, now
beholds with becoming pride his three sons in as many
different corps of volunteers ! Posterity will not fail
to appreciate the obligations under which she has
been laid by the " rifle movement " of the present time,
and will, doubtless, give it perpetuation. We, what-

ever betide, will unmistakenly hold sacred " deck and
shore," and wisdom predominating (by His Divine Will)
in all our counsels, there will be perceived in us no
diminution of " martial " or patriotic ardour.

In this little volume the English versions have been
arranged in that order in which it seemed best for the
general reader to entertain them. Part II. will con-
tain the Greek originals, and the Latin translations
by the " great " Grotius. A specimen of the translation, executed in 1761, is placed in an Appendix. For
a singular specimen of translation from Tyrtœus, the
curious reader is referred to "Gent. Mag.," vol. xv.,
p. 587. For the " Martial Elegy," and the " Martial
Address," the translator must entirely throw himself
upon the indulgence of the reader, who may be inclined,
regarding it (the former) merely as an humble tribute
(amongst ten thousand others) to a great and good man,
to bestow a wish that it had been "worthier " the
theme it attempts to celebrate.

SUBSCRIBERS.

1. The Most Noble His Grace the DUKE OF DEVON-SHIRE, K.G., Chancellor of the University of Cambridge.
2. The Right Hon. Lord Justice K. BRUCE. *Six copies.*
3. The Right Hon. the Earl of CLARENDON, K.G.
4. The Right Hon. Lord ELCHO, M.P.
5. The Most Hon. the Marquess of LANSDOWNE, K.G.
6. The Right Hon. and Right Rev. the LORD BISHOP of LONDON.
7. The Right Hon. LORD LYNDHURST, High Steward of the University of Cambridge.
8. The Right Hon. Lord MONTEAGLE. *Two copies.*
9. The Right Hon. Lord Viscount PALMERSTON, K.G.
10. Sir ROUNDELL PALMER, Deputy-Steward of the University of Oxford.
11. The Right Hon. the Earl of SHAFTESBURY. *Sixteen copies.*
12. The Right Hon. the Earl of ZETLAND.
13. DIGBY C. WRANGHAM, Esq., Q.C. *Ten copies.*
14. DIXON ROBINSON, Esq., Clitheroe Castle, Clitheroe. *Three copies.*
15. MATTHEW ARNOLD, Esq., M.A., Professor of Poetry, Oriel College, Oxford.

16. Rev. J. Bond, M.A., Vicar of Weston, near Bath.
17. Rev. Joseph Bosworth, D.D., Professor of Anglo-Saxon, Christ Church, Oxford.
18. Henry Calley, Esq., Burderop Park, near Swindon, Wilts.
19. John W. Clark, Esq., M.A., Trinity College, Cambridge.
20. N. H. Clifton, Esq., Islington.
21. Rev. Alexander Dyce, M.A.
22. John Elliotson, Esq., M.D., Cantab. F.R.S.
23. Rev. John Glover, M.A., Librarian of Trinity College, Cambridge.
24. Edwin Guest, LL.D., Master of Gonville and Caius College, Cambridge. *Two copies.*
25. J. H. Gurney, Esq., M.P. *Two copies.*
26. Rev. R. W. Jelf, D.D., Canon of Christ Church, and Principal of King's College, London.
27. Rev. Benjamin Jowett, M.A., Regius Professor of Greek, Balliol College, Oxford. *Two copies.*
28. Rev. John Lamb, M.A., Hulsean Lecturer, Gonville and Caius College, Cambridge. *Four copies.*
29. Very Rev. Henry G. Liddell, D.D., Dean of Christ Church, Oxford.
30. Rev. J. R. Major, D.D., Head Master of King's College School. *Four copies.*
31. Rev. G. F. Mortimer, D.D., Head Master of the City of London School.
32. C. A. Macintosh, Esq. *Two copies.*
33. Rev. W. Martin, M.A., Vicar of Grantchester, near Cambridge.
34. James E. Boggis, Esq. *Two copies.*
35. Rev. T. Boggis, Aldborough, near York.
36. C. Burls, Esq.
37. E. Grant Burls, Esq. *Two copies.*
38. W. Smithers, Esq.

39. J. H. MARKLAND, D.C.L., F.R.S., S.A., Bath.
40. Rev. EMILIUS NICHOLSON, Minsterly, Salop.
41. THEOPHILUS NICHOLSON, Esq.
42. SAMUEL PHELPS, Esq., Canonbury.
43. Professor PRYME, Cambridge. *Six copies.*
44. Rev. ADAM SEDGWICK, M.A., Professor of Geology, Trinity College, Cambridge. *Two copies.*
45. Rev. E. J. SELWYN, M.A., Head Master of Blackheath Proprietary School.
46. L. C. SPENCER, Esq., Queen's Road, Dalston.
47. CHARLES TUCKETT, Esq., British Museum.
48. EDWARD TAYLOR, Esq., Professor of Music, Gresham College.
49. Rev. W. H. THOMPSON, M.A., Regius Professor of Greek, Trinity College, Cambridge.

MARTIAL ADDRESS

TO THE BRITISH VOLUNTEERS.

—◇—

1.

Hail, gallant youths, Britannia's darling pride !
How promptly ye arose at honour's call ;
And with heroic ardour, side by side
Prepared to stand, and, if need were, to fall !

2.

5 The patriotic deed through Europe rings ;
E'en they who envy, or who hate, admire
Strongly the warmth with which each Briton clings
To native shores unharm'd by hostile ire.

3.

Nations at length by sad experience wise,
10 And tutor'd by your own example bright,
Shall learn sweet Peace, and happy homes, to prize,
And stand but in defence of Freedom's right.

4.

Meantime learn ye the lore that Mars can teach,
Fierce grasp the steel, search each strategic wile ;
15 Should subtlety then seek to overreach,
Ye well may beat him back with all his guile.

5.

Dread not to hear on bayonet bayonet jar ;
Retiring, scorn thick deaths by hand unseen ;
If in the square ye mingle in the war,
20 Remember what your ancestors have been.

6.

Unto the harsh command obedience yield,
Be it to march into the vale of death,—
Where grape and canister plough up the field,
And chymic art empoisons vital breath.

7.

25 O, dire the onslaught, deep the wound should be,
Where'er invader lifts his haughty head !
Such caitiff, heav'n, thrust back into the sea,
With monsters of the deep to make his bed.

8.

Our sacred hearths, our wives, our children dear,
30 Our good intentions, all our hearts inspire,
And, whilst we other nations' rights revere,
Prompt us to animate our martial fire.

9.

' Ye gentlemen of England, bold yeomen !'
What deeds of high emprize remain untold,
35 The British race hath not achieved ? agen
What shall they not achieve then as of old ?

10.

Say, who first carried sail the world around ?
Who in the Arctic clime new passage sought ?
Who burst the prison gate, erst bolted found,
40 And to enlighten'd Europe knowledge brought ?

11.

Where doth the fetter, as by magic, fall,
Erecting the dark human form divine ?
The nations round best know ; and, one and all,
Witness in you the antique spirit shine.

12.

45 Hail then, brave youths, Britannia's hopeful pride !
From Cambria, and from Scotia, trooping come ;
Nor let the seas Ierne's love divide,—
One VICTORY for all, or else one Tomb !

I.

MARTIAL FRAGMENT OF TYRTÆUS.

(B.C. 682.)

Τεθνάμεναι γὰρ καλὸν κ.τ.λ.

———◆———

1.

How comely fall in the front-ranks the brave,
  Who for dear father-land their dear life sell !
But to abandon country will not save
  From indigence, of evils the most fell.

2.

5 Nor matron staid, nor thy good sire's great age,
  Nor infant pale, nor spotless wife's sad face,
Shall screen thee from the hard world's hate and
    rage,
  If Penury and grizzling Want have place.

3.

Such wretched wand'rer lineage high doth shame,
10 And noble form, whilst every ill draws near ;
Nor yearns his spirit now, dead to honest fame,
  To make the captive of the bow and spear.

4.

Then let us fight with all our might and main,
  Die for our sons, nor spare our heart's rich stream.
15 And ye, brave youths, close-marshall'd on the plain,
  Account base flight and fear an idle dream.

5.

Make ye a mighty heart, and val'rous soul,
 Fear not in hurtling with the foe to bleed ;
And if the veteran in the dry dust roll
20 (Weak were his knees), bestride him in his need.

6.

For, Oh the shame, in the fore rank to find
 With snow-white head, and beard all hoary grey,
The old man spoil'd, and, for ye lagg'd behind,
 Breathing, alas, his gallant soul away !

7.

25 Sweet Youth ! hard doom beseems thy flow'ry tide,
 Retaining yet soft fragrancy and bloom,
By Valour courted, and by Beauty's pride,
 E'en lovelier still within the silent tomb.

II.

MARTIAL FRAGMENT OF TYRTÆUS.

'Αλλ' 'Ηρακλῆος γὰρ ἀνικήτου κ.τ.λ.

———◦◦◦———

1.

NE'ER deem your arms grown weak, or hearts
    wax'd cold,
But right against the foe advance the shield.
Not yet doth Jove his look averted hold,
    And great Alcides' race ne'er leave the field.

2.

5 Be dear alike, where issues fitful are,
    Death's murky gloom, or Day's bright golden
    beam :
Full well ye know the temper of grim War,
    And how exploits be sprent with Sorrow's stream.

3.

In full career of victory oft ye slew,
10   And dire reverse oft number'd thick your slain.
Again in conflict close, men good and true,
    Dare side by side stout combat to maintain.

4.

Thus fewer fall, rear-ranks in safety move,
    Eke most imposing doth such valour show.
15 But whom death shakes, or dangers recreant prove,
    He dire disgrace, and countless ills, shall know.

5.

Ah, grief! that foe should lacerate behind
  The coward hide that flees ou martial ground.
Ah, shame! that his dead corse the brave should
    find
20 Exhibiting in front no glorious wound.

6.

Then stand, determination firm express'd,
  Fix'd to the soil where Freedom loves to be.
Each screen his thighs, legs, shoulders, and broad
    chest,
  Opposing buckler's wide convexity.

7.

25 Each in his right hand shake the thund'ring spear:
  Nod, dreadful plume, on helm, nod high o'er all!
The lore that Mars can teach learn now: nor fear
  To tread where arrows thickest whiz or fall.

8.

Dare near approach, the foeman fiercely charge,
30   And grapple with him for the mastery:
Foot to foot, casque to casque, targe match'd with
    targe,
  Confront the caitiff wheresoe'r he be.

9.

And ye, light-harness'd, for the skirmish meet,
  Ranged in length, crouch'd 'neath the buckler
    bright,
35 With pond'rous stones and darts the stranger greet,
  Fenced by the heavy phalanx mail'd in might.

III.

MARTIAL FRAGMENT OF TYRTÆUS.

Οὐτ᾽ ἂν μνησαίμην, κ.τ.λ.

1.

No chronicle, devote to SPARTA's fame,
   No fair word whisper'd in LACONIA's ear,
Shall mark thee worthy thy ancestral name,
   By Mavors honour'd, or to Venus dear ;

2.

5 Swift though thy foot, as erst Achilles', fly,
   Though Hercules his match at wrestling find ;
With Cyclops though in size and strength thou vie,
   And in the run outstrip the *Thracian wind :—

3.

Nor though Tithonus' stature yield in grace,
10   Or Midas, Cinyras, thou in gold excel ;
Or thou than Pelops have more regal space,
   Or have Adrastus' tongue, sweet-dropping well:—

4.

If thou, though giv'n each glory 'neath the sky,
   Which stamps with lustre, or ennoble can,
15 Yet shrink'st in gory battle-field to try
   The sword's keen edge upon the hostile man.

---

* Viz. the North wind, as in respect of SPARTA.

5.

Ay, this is VALOUR, meed 'mongst men most high,
  The fairest gift for youthful pride to wear :
A good alike to the community,
20   The good alike city and people share !

6.

Lo, where he stedfast in the front rank fights,
  Heedless of dastard flight, exposing life,
Comrade exhorting FOR OUR COUNTRY'S RIGHTS :
  This man is gallant in the warlike strife !

7.

25 Eftsoons his valour the rough phalanx brake,
   His zeal hath stemm'd the battle's raging tide ;
Now fall'n in the fore rank FOR COUNTRY'S SAKE
   His death gives fame to SPARTA far and wide,

8.

And to his village home, and rustic sire.
30   Oft pierced through breast, and oft through bossy
     shield,
And oft through mail in front, he did expire,
   And now low lies wrapp'd in ensanguin'd field.

9.

Him the whole city mourns with deep regret ;
  Both old and young with tears gaze on his tomb.
35 Nor ever dies the fair renown ; nor yet
  His name. His children famous do become,

10.

His children's children, and the unborn race.
  Such honour waits the bold, the brave, the true,
Who DIE FOR SACRED HEARTHS in duty's place,
40   Bright immortality their guerdon due.

11.

Now should he 'scape death's drowsy-lengthsome
    hour,
  And with his spear achieve a victor's meeds,
Youth and old age fresh laurels on him shower,
  And wreath'd with joys his useful life proceeds.

12.

45 Bow'd down at length by TIME, who bows down all,
  Revered, distinguish'd, girt with truthful friends,
The young make way for him in public hall,
  The elders, and his old compeers. Descends

13.

The HERO thus, to sleep in GLORY's arms.
50   Fame's pinnacles to reach, with fierce desire
Breathes there a SPARTAN whose proud soul not
    warms ?
  Why, then, ACHIEVE, nor slack your martial
    fire !

IV.

MARTIAL FRAGMENT ASCRIBED TO
*CALLINUS.

Μέχρις τεῦ κατάκεισθε ; κ.τ λ.

—————◦⬦◦——

1.

How long will ye in idlesse waste away
  The precious time ? nor deed of valour try ?
Nor blush while they who dwell around survey
  Your virtue slack'ning thus exceedingly ?

2.

5 Deem ye these are the times of piping peace ?
  Awake, I say ; and rouse your gallant soul ;
For War that trampleth down ignoble Ease,
  Throughout the land like one broad flame doth
    roll.

3.

Now is the time with skill to couch the spear,
10 Now is the time to push the shield with power,
To fight, all gash'd and maim'd, the foeman near,
  To the last moment of your dying hour.

4.

Fair fame is theirs, who from invading foe
  SAVE COUNTRY, SONS, and fresh-ywedded WIFE !
15 With spear and shield then boldly 'gainst him go,
  Soon as the din proclaims the mingled strife.

* Attributed by some to Callimachus.

5.

And since DETH comes to all, when he will come,
    And MANNE may not his stern decree eschew,
Though gods be his progenitors ; such doom
20   'Count glorious on the battle-field ; and rue

6.

Pale death at home.   From clatter, arms, and scars,
    Escaped, seek not on couch to yield your breath :
This brings no honour to the son of Mars,
    But Veneration weeps o'er gallant death.

7.

25 Grandly he falls in arms of VICTORY,
    Whose godlike form aye watch'd at honour's post.
A tower of strength he plainly seem'd to be,
    And, singly, oft bewray'd himself AN HOST !

MARTIAL ELEGY

On the Demise of

H. R. H. Prince Albert.

———◆◇◆———

I. 1.

FALL'N is that column, sweet and fair to see,
Which whilere did uphold in lovely wise
The golden architrave of social weal,
With all the joyous bright entablature.
Fall'n is the column. Oh, full many a flower
Of rich expectancy lies crush'd below
The beauteous weight ! Bloom shall they never more,
Nor that proud column rear again its head
9 Where human hand, or mortal eye, have power.
   Ye rustic maids, who while away the hour
A-culling nature's wild weeds, whence, 'tis said,
With elegant forms your truthful minds ye store,
And teach them to your fairy handiwork,
Are ye too sad ? and, mournful in your mood,
For sorrowing cypress change ye lilies fair,
For myrtle eglantine ? Ah, well I know
The doleful ditty from dear bosom welling
18 Sadly your sympathy, gently your grief, is telling !

I. 2.

Approach, and fear ye not ; but on this bank
(Which laurel shades) together let us sit,

And mingle griefs, and drop the pearly tear;
So nature finds relief, and placid calm.
So by the river-side the captives wept,
Remembering Zion. And they hang'd their harps
'Upon the willows in the midst thereof,'
Nor deign'd to soothe their sufferings with song,
27 Since in strange land the waster with them kept.
    We, nor from homestead, nor from freedom, swept.
The dire mishap, irreparable, long
Remembering, where no man will jeer and scoff,
Both now and eft our 'chief joy' will take down,
And bid attention to its tuneful strings:
A mournful air shall start our tears afresh,
A muffled rhyme shall oft our tears renew,
A martial strain at length shall solace bring,
36 Nor my right hand forget 'her cunning,' while we
    sing.

I. 3.

Ah, well could he unlock sweet Music's source,
And bid her luscious streams flow far and wide,
Enchanting homes! Himself too knew to sing,
And weave the magic weft of poesy.
Enriching Thought's domain. The sisters boon,
Painting, who lends to colour form and life,
And Sculpture, who bids Beauty soft and warm
Step from the marble block, knew him their friend;
45 Whilst Learning gave, 'twas all she could, one
    throne.
    Nor less did Science mark him for her own,
Bright Science, whose fair footsteps heav'nward
    tend,
Whom young Invention courts. Her wieldy arm
Lightly she casts o'er many a land remote;
By her the spark talks 'neath th' Atlantic roar;

The dark Earth yields to Day a sheeny house,
In which is holden the big World's vast fair ;
The rock is broken ; forth pure water wells ;
54 Truth beams, and Ignorance foul, like hated cloud.
    dispels !

I. 4.

Yet what avails it that the child of clay
Divulge the laws earth's crust which regulate,
Developing by study night and day
The mineral wealth that makes a nation great ?
He may discover, but shall ne'er *create* :
Nor, though with him the chymic wonders bring
(Whose art shall ne'er make *void* the smallest seed).
Can his voice back recall the spirit ta'en wing,—
63 As now with him, for whom our hearts do bleed.

    Then lowly bend, thou seer, in learned cell,
And meditate on man's most weak estate ;
It were a theme we oft should ponder well,
To curb swoll'n pride, or spirits too much elate.
With resignation and with pious will
Each dire bereavement firmly must be borne,
And the pale sorrowing cheek be wiped; yet still
Be often wet. Remembrance is a thorn
72 Near Eden's bow'r that grew, beloved, though it
    hath torn.

II. 1.

Befits us here to pause, and change our style,
Pierian maidens, deck'd in raiment bright.
Next celebrate with martial minstrelsy
The hero lost, who was both good and great.
He came ; in youth's fresh fragrance, bold and free,
With glory at his heart. And much he yearn'd
To win a chaplet for himself ; and stand

To all posterity a brilliant light,
81 And grand exemplar of what man should be.
    He came ; and England's beauty flock'd to see :
The veteran too was there with eager sight ;
The babe sprang forth, and stretch'd its little hand,
Which now, e'en now, to manhood's goal arrived,
Wields the sharp steel with patriotic glow.
All, all were fill'd with wonder and delight,
To see that youth, now wrapt in darksome shade,
With rapid wheels to Glory's field careering ;
90 Raised was the loyal arm, and loud the gladsome
    cheering.

II. 2.

In fields of Love the battle first he won,
And show'd himself a mighty conqueror.
Not Cæsar's self an equal glory knew ;
Not Ammon's son, self-styled, whom men call
    great.
Though ransack'd be the old historic page,
Where bloodshed, rapine, winged words describe :
Though each exploit the Grecian stage held dear
Be scann'd ; unmatch'd, and matchless, will remain
99 His name, and famed in every future age.
    To high embattled towers, proof 'gainst Time's
        rage,
Where ancient forest waves o'er spacious plain,
The gazing multitudes beheld him bear,
Like antique warrior, regal bride away,
Rare virtue's meed.   From that time forth he
    framed
Grand schemes to benefit his fellow-man.
For lofty was the tenour of his mind,
As is the eagle's flight in fields of air ;
108 As noiseless eke,—since good, not praise, was all
    his care.

II. 3.

And heaven did greatly bless the meek and just,
As onward he pursued his bright career ;
And God did build his house ; so not in vain
He hasted to the work at early dawn,
Reluctant quitted at still voice of eve.
When from the Lord a gift and heritage
Befell : lo, hath he not his quiver fill'd
With radiant arrows ? round the parent stem,
117 The children of his youth their branches weave !
   O doom'd this earthly scene so soon to leave !
Thy counsel we should oft miss, save for them,
Whom thou in virtue's lore hast wisely skill'd,
To be our comfort. They, if need should be,
Will in the gate speak sharply with the foe,
Or milder and more kindly method use,
With unabashèd front, and forehead high,
Enlustring thy great name. O well is thee ;
126 Bright path was thine illumed by immortality !

II. 4.

Can we forget that face serenely bold,
O'er which the plume so gaily wont to dance,
Whene'er him list a martial field to hold,
And proudly on his glorious war-steed prance ?
Behold the veterans with firm step advance,
Red is their coat, and sable is their crest,
And steel-tipp'd is the weapon in their hand,
And love of country thrills in every breast,
135 For which full oft they fall in foreign land.
   Alas, no more he heads the gallant train,
His faithful charger knows his voice no more,
His servants not expect him home again,
The day's great business, and the field, being o'er !

Yet still the veterans with their proud step march,
And love of country fires each noble heart,
Whilst thou far, far beyond high heaven's arch,
Hast gone to glory, where no more they part,
144 Where tears be dried, and balm is pour'd on sor-
        row's smart.

III. 1.

Ay me ! how hard it is to wean our thought
From that which hath familiar been so long ;
Or bring belief, though by sharp lesson taught,
To credit change in aught that seemèd strong !
Can he be gone, so lately us among ?
There stand the elms in childhood's hour we
        knew,
There reigns the oak, whence we the chaplet
        pull'd,
There blooms the cowslip pale, where erst it blew ;
153 The lovely scene, 'tis true, seems somewhat lull'd.
    The lilies too, our olden friends, are there ;
Still babbles o'er the stones the silver brook ;
'Tis true, old faces scantily appear,
And wear a worn and more expressive look.
Far other children sport upon the plain ;
A novel youth robust delights in arms !
Scan we this page in nature's book again,
For whilst 'sweet home' my anxious bosom charms,
162 This change which here hath chanced my inmost
        soul alarms.

III. 2.

Tell me, thou antique spire, for thou must know,
Continually shifts thus the village scene ?
—Yes ! imperceptibly they come, they go ;
Impossible the track where they have been :

Yet here the ivy, there the yew-tree green.—
Speak, pebble, from the crusted stone-arch rent,
For thou art elder by a million years,
And both by wind and wave hast oft been sent
171 Whirling ; know'st aught of man, his joys, his tears ?
   —Yes ! casting angle, the poor fisher sigh'd,
Who first me took, then gave unto the stream ;
The sportive infant next me gladly eyed,
O'er whose drown'd form the midnight moonbeams
    gleam ;
The arm'd one with the sling lent wings to me,
And laugh'd, soon doom'd to bleed, when blood he
    drew :
None e'er their time knew, nor what time mote be.
Together now they sleep 'neath shade of yew,—
180 The mason eke, who wrought with square and
    plummet true.—

III. 3.

Haste then, to arms ! to glorious arms divine !
The shield of faith, the Spirit's all-conqu'ring
    sword,
Salvation's helmet ! on your breast let shine
The plate of righteousness ! strong in the Lord,
And in the might and power of his Word !
Since high and low so lightly pass away,
Guard we our jewel, our eternal joy !
For them we fear not, who can only slay :
189 Them tempest's wrath can scatter and destroy.
   So arm'd went forth (ere evening clouds descend)
The faithful consort, and the father dear,
The fosterer of arts, the orphan's friend,
Who for fall'n warrior ne'er refused a tear.
So loved, so wept, hath hero seldom been,
Who long at honour's post hath faithful stood.

And now far greater bliss he holds, I ween,
Than grand Destroyer, stained with guiltless
blood.
198 Oh, he is truly great who shames not to be good !

III. 4.

THE EARTH AND THE EARTH'S FULNESS IS THE
LORD'S !

Ye nations, learn in whom our faith we place,
And change for pruning-hooks your temper'd
swords,
And seek the love of God, and His Son's grace ;
Then Liberty shall shine in every place.
Whilst England's sons their Sabbath bell observe,
Sweet peace shall bless each town and village
green ;
Long as from toil and duty they not swerve,
207 Happy her beauteous daughters shall be seen.
Rise then, oh rise, thou regal pile, on high,
To speak for ALBERT to a future age,
And speak for her, whose hope is in the sky!
Adjust for him the speech, ye statesmen sage ;
Attune for her the voice, ye poets bold.
Lo, bard, and statesman, and high pillar rent,
Shall by Decay in kindred dust be roll'd,
Ere the fair wreaths, Affection's tribute lent,
216 Wither and fade away, or lose their holy scent !

APPENDIX.

I.

---◇---

I would not praise the man, his deeds rehearse,
Nor e'en make mention of his name in verse,
That's fam'd for mighty feats in wrestling shewn,
Or for the prizes that his speed has won :
Not tho' he equal to the Cyclops rise, 5
In nervous limbs, and huge gigantic size ;
Not tho' he spring so nimbly o'er the field,
That vanquish'd Boreas to his swiftness yield ;
Tho' he surpass Tithonus' graceful mien,
In just proportion, and in look serene : 10
Tho' he possess of wealth a larger store
Than Phrygian Midas, or than Cinyras more ;
Or tho' a monarch he more sceptres hold
Than mighty Pelops bore in times of old ;
Tho' on his lips yet sweeter accents hung 15
Than flow'd persuasive from Adrastus' tongue ;
With ev'ry virtue tho' completely blest,
If valour add not lustre to the rest.
 For none can boast a brave and valiant heart,
And in the fight maintain a hero's part, 20
Unless he fearless, and intrepid bear
To view the bloody carnage of the war ;

And with impatient fury burn to close
And foot to foot attack his rushing foes.
This is a man's best, greatest, noblest praise, 25
And shall to youth immortal glory raise.
True is that soldier, faithful to defend
His country's cause, his people's common friend,
Himself who hazards life, and standing nigh
Exhorts his comrade that he bravely die. 30
This, this is he can boast a valiant heart,
And in the fight maintain a hero's part.

 Himself he turns th' embattled foe to flight,
And stems the torrent of th' unequal fight.
Ennobling friends, house, parents, as he dies, 35
Soon 'midst the first a breathless corse he lies;
With many a glorious wound transfix'd before,
His shield and breastplate stain'd with flowing gore.
The aged mourn, the youth their joys forego,
And all the city join in common woe. 40
His children's children, and those yet to come,
Shall reap fresh honours from their parent's tomb.
What, tho' his ashes lie entomb'd? his name
Shall gain unbounded, and eternal fame,
Who, in his children's and his country's right, 45
Exerts his utmost efforts in the fight;
Maintains his stand with honour, joins the strife,
And to dread Mars's fury yields his life.

 But should not death, involv'd in endless night
Snatch him for ever from the realms of light; 50
Should he, successful in his bloody toils,
Return in triumph, crown'd with glorious spoils,

To him both young and old due honours pay,
And endless pleasures bless his latest day.
What time he ranks the agèd sires among,   55
He's still distinguish'd from th' ignoble throng.
'Gainst him no villain harbours envious rage,
Justice, and fear of shame protect his age.
And when the Senate in full council meet,
To him all orders rising leave their seat.   60
   O! then let all to this high summit soar
Of valour, nor abate the thirst of war.

RICHARD BARRETT, PRINTER, MARK LANE, LONDON.

www.ingramcontent.com/pod-product-compliance
Lightning Source LLC
Chambersburg PA
CBHW021442090426
42739CB00009B/1609